DOPE
FIENDS
Daughter

THE
DAVIDA WOOTEN
STORY

Arranged, written, produced and associated
Published by

Jullian Smallwood

Certified Publisher

ISBN SOFTCOVER 978-164921342-6

This Book is Dedicated to/ and in Loving memories of

Bobbie Smith

David Wooten Jr.

Baron Smith

Robert Wooten

Rayquan Elliot

Aka

"Stack Bundles"

Joyce Cotman

Toya Cotman

Ethel Butler

Rebecca Hayes

Gem D'Amato

Sal Seidel

Doris Wolkin

Emily Collington

Tawana Scott

Intro

Through the lies, deception, hate, hurt, pain and the drugs. Through it all, I'm still standing.

What don't kill me, makes me stronger!

This is my story...

Chapter 1

Born on one of the busiest days of the year. And no, it was not Christmas eve or Christmas day, or the 4th of July.

Hours prior to the time of the dropping of the ball in Times Square, in New York City, a baby girl was born.

On December 31, 1966, Bobbie Jean and David Wooten gave birth to a baby girl, in Peninsular hospital in Far Rockaway, Queens, in the state of New York.

This was Bobbie's second out of what would eventually be 6 children, who would be 3 boys and 3 girls. My father had 4 boys and 4 girls.

I had twin brothers, one resembles me and my mom. The other looked more like his father.

My mother and father met in Harlem U.S.A. She was working as a housekeeper. More like cleaning white people houses.

She would sing in night clubs. She song periodically throughout her life. Even when she was strung out on dope.

They hooked up. They moved over by Riverside drive, in Harlem.

She got pregnant with me. She moved to far rockaway Queens. Dad remained in Harlem. He lived off 145th Street, on Amsterdam Avenue and Convent Avenue.

My Father wanted a boy, but the universe did not agree with that. Instead, he was blessed with a daughter. His response to that was he decided to name me Davida.

So, there you have it. That is how my name came about. For those of you, who did not get it?

Simple, yet clever. My name is Davida, David with an a, added to it. I was a bowlegged, big-eyed baby girl.

My earliest years I was known for my big cheeks and for biting people.

My bowlegs issues became a serious issue when I began to walk. It was so severe by the time I was 4, I was issued leg braces to help with that problem.

Being bowlegged was one of the things I inherited from my father, for sure. wearing them leg braces made my legs nice, firm and strong. It is like, it went from a negative to a positive.

Later, in life my legs would play a definite part in the way my body would eventually look. If I can remember money was not a problem in my life. We were not poor.

We were not rich either. We were what they describe as being hood rich. Which means, money was constantly coming in and out of the household.

Money was always moving. Something I really did not notice or cared about at the time.

At the time I had no clue that I would be participating in any of it at all. Well, that is what I thought?

My mother also was a natural born hustler. That was one lady who knew how to make some money. She was incredibly good at it. She made money doing hair.

I remember watching her sometimes while she did someone's hair. Saturday afternoon, sitting in my mom's kitchen in the Redfern housing Projects in Far rockaway.

Fan blowing hot air through-out our small project apartment. When the hot comb was not in use, she lay the iron part on a lit eye on the stove. To keep the hot comb, hot.

This is what she used to give perms to the needy. It did not stop there, my mother also did piercings, Ears, noses, and whatever else needed to be pierce.

We saw it all living in my mother's household. My mother even delivered quite a few babies on our Livingroom floor.

You know the old saying, he is a jack of all traits. In her case, she was a Jane of all traits. My mother was always an excellent cook.

She was from Alabama. Everyone from her neck of the woods knew how to throwdown in the kitchen.

Naturally, she taught me and my sister how to cook. I could tell you one thing, I know for sure, I could cook some grits. She made me cook grits, repeatedly.

I must be an excellent grits maker. A grits specialist. She would send me on so many random occasions back to the kitchen multiple times to make some damn grits.

She sent us back no matter how many times until we got her grits right. She wanted it prepared her way. Only her way of making grits.

She would instruct us to prepare her grits using a big wooden folk. Instead of the conventional way with a big wooden spoon. She always stated by preparing this way it avoids lumps in the grits.

Music was the soundtrack to my life. Most of my memory exist with me being around my mother.

I really did not know much of my father back then, to be honest. He was around every now and again.

The last thing I mostly remembered about him was he promised me a bike for my 9th birthday. That never happened and I never did learn how to ride a bike.

My dad was in noticeably different periods in my life. Every time I saw him, I would remind him of the bike I never got. This went on all the way up until his death. To my surprise, he left me his inheritance.

My stepmother and my mother got cool. Then they started getting high together. Early on my stepmother would sew me nice dresses. She was good at it. She always treated me like I was one of her own kids. I really liked that.

She used dope. She didn't do the crack thing. I know for a fact I got a lot of her ways. She would never place a random man ahead of her children.

Even my father experienced that with my stepmother. My mother was the opposite when it came down to priorities, my mother would sit there and make the man of her life for the moment some steak and potatoes.

While we her children ate leftovers. If any of my stepmother's guy friends would argue with one of her kids.

She would be ready to kick somebody's behind over her babies. She was no joke when it came down to her babies.

I got a lot of my gold digger's ways from my God mother Maria Shivers. How she worked men to get what she wanted.

She was a professional at it. It was like dudes lined up to trick on her. I saw her get things from men that you wouldn't even believe.

She broke a lot of men hearts.

Chapter 2

From such a calm, peaceful baby with little to no worries. I grew into a spoiled brat. An uncontrollable kid. It got so out of hand, to the point of me being expelled from school in the 4th grade.

I had major behavioral issues. Teachers and students alike were intimidated by my antics.

After that they placed me in a six hundred school. Placed me in special education, not because of my grades. All because of my attitude and behavior.

God always provided a lane through the madness. This would go continuously throughout my life. Even to this day.

Like in this situation, At the six hundred school I met two great black female teachers. Ms. Daniels and Ms. Frankel took me under their wing and guided me.

Ms. Daniels helped me get out of special ed. Back into regular mainstream classes. Once they assured me that I was somebody.

That led me to stop picking on other students. And disrupting classes those teachers were teaching.

Once I learn all of that I got re-evaluated. Now, I know you are wondering, how I got from there to there.

My mother was a hard-working woman. She would save her money in her bank account she had at the Jamaica saving bank on Mott Avenue.

Well, let me explain how all of this went down. Like I stated before life started simple and ordinary for me.

Then the day happened that would forever change my life. In more ways than one. My mother's man came into the picture.

We were in our project building waiting for the elevator to reach our floor. The elevator opens and we see three black men in the process of robbing a white man.

My siblings and I were scared. My mother pushes us along into the elevator. The men took the white guy off the elevator. My mother told us to hurry up and mind our business.

We did not know what was going on. Or the fact that my mother and one of the guys caught eye contact.

When we heard the story later that day. The three guys robbed the insurance man. Back then the insurance guy would carry large amounts of money on them at times.

So yes, the insurance man and the milk man were absolute targets for stickup guys. Some felt like it was an inside job.

it was not even the half of the shocker. About 2 weeks later at the time, she was starting a relationship with one of the guys who robbed the insurance guy that day.

 We knew who he was. We reminded our mother of the fact, that guy was one of the men the other day on the elevator.

She looked at us and said, No! She changes the subject behind that. Even though she damn well knew it was him. We gave her this look like who you are fooling.

Already it was crazy. Crazy will be an understatement as you shall find out. My mother's new man of her life at the time name was Ike.

Just like that my stepfather enters our lives. For the better and worst. That is a real statement right there. That changed everything.

Because that is when the drugs got involved. My mom got strung out. This roller coaster they call life began officially at that point for me.

My mother changed dramatically. She started hanging with a new group of people. Her whole attitude changes.

She would not attend Parent, Teacher conference. She would send me instead. Even though I was dressed kind of grown.

But clearly, they had to see I was a child myself.

We always had on the latest. When it came down to what clothes we wore.

She stopped working. All her and her friends did was stay locked in her bedroom getting high. I remember one time when my mother and stepfather got into a heated argument.

My step pops left out of the room. He didn't feel like carrying on with the argument. My mother runs out the bedroom after him.

My mother forgot she had a rag tied around her arm. My sister and I sat there devastated over what we just witnessed.

Till this day, I don't close any doors in my house. Only the bathroom door when I'm using it.

I don't like a smokey smelling place. I always kept a neat clean apartment. I like everything white with glass.

Chapter 3

My mother's boyfriend Ike, despite it all. Out of all the men my mother dealt with, I only considered Ike as my stepfather.

First, he was around us the longest. He was there for almost a decade. Until one day this white guy from Cedarhurst messed up the money.

The guy from Cedarhurst was well dressed and neat. That was the reason he was able to ask for credit on some dope. They thought he would be able to pay it back.

With drugs and drug addicts nothing ever goes as planned. They found out that he couldn't afford to pay his debt. My step pops took it personal.

He really didn't like the fact the guy did not come up with the money. Even after a warning. Ike got one of his Puerto Rican homeboys and they both went to pay this man a visit.

Ike and his buddy JR went to the man's house to rob him. They tied him up. When the man was able to get himself loose.

Ike and JR were far gone. But the damage was done. After freeing himself the man quickly called the authorities.

Shortly afterwards, Ike and JR were arrested.

They were sent to jail. Then they were convicted and sentenced to 8 years in prison. We used to visit Ike while he was housed on Riker's Island.

When he was shipped up north, my mother started dealing with other men. She started a new relationship with one of her clients.

His name was Smokey. He was the worst. He made me sick. He thought he was the man of the house. My mother always took her boyfriends' side. Instead of her own children.

He was short and well built. He also was extremely cocky. He always found it necessary to give all the customers a hard time. Especially if they came short with the money.

He was a nightmare. He made it very difficult to get money around him. He was something else. When my mother talks to her friends. He would insert himself into their conversation.

He would write her love letters while she's on the phone. He was a very annoying and controlling man.

We mainly sold dope. Smokie was into speed balling. That is when he mixes coke and dope together.

He had to go and buy some cocaine. If he wanted some coke. He brought the coke. He mixed the two drugs.

After he already got high. And then suddenly, he didn't like the cocaine. So, he went back to confront the guy who sold him the coke.

He flips out on the guy. He tells the guy the cocaine he sold to him was garbage.

Then he went on to threatening the drug dealer. After humiliating the guy on the street.

Smokie leaves and heads back to the project building. The drug dealer follows him back. Smokie started it. Little did he know the drug dealer was going to finish it.

Smokie went into the building. He ran to catch the elevator. At this same time my neighbor little Rodney was on the elevator too. He was around 9 years old at the time.

The guy opened fire. He shot up the elevator, hitting Smokie several times. Bullets were fired. Smokie died that day in the elevator.

Even though the little boy didn't get hit. Thank God for that. Still, the young man was traumatized over the events that took place.

My neighbor son was never the same after what he had witnessed. I was at the movies with friends when all of this had taken place. Something told me to call home.

My mother answered the phone in tears. I could tell by her voice. She was clearly upset because of what transpired.

She was crying and she instructed me to take the other kids upstairs by using the stairwell. After that day we never saw that drug dealer ever again.

I'm might sound a little crazy. But I was glad the guy got away and didn't have to go to jail.

For one, he was a very cool person. He just handled his business. He wasn't out to bother anyone. Okie started that beef.

He hustled his cocaine. Very humble person. 3 months later, my mother moves another man into the house. This new guy was another piece of work.

His name was Charles. He thought he was the man of all men. You know the highest of the high. I couldn't stand him. Just as much as I couldn't stand Smokie.

Chapter 4

My mother was a functionable dope fiend. After she was introduced to the drugs by my step-pops.

My mother was a natural born hustler, she would eventually be known for selling all types of drugs and narcotics.

I do not like using irons to this day. Because my mother used to make us iron her boyfriend jeans. His 22 pairs of dungarees.

All 22 pairs had to be iron properly. And she would inspect the dungarees to make sure you did not miss a spot. Also, to see if you caught all the wrinkles. That used to annoy me.

Nowadays either I would take certain garments to the cleaners to be washed and ironed. Besides that, I am basic, I just wear wrinkle free clothing.

Mainly packages of heroin and cocaine. My mother was affiliated with. Memories of bringing people back around from a drug overdose.

I used things that I saw my mother use when she was trying to revive someone from an overdose.

I used things like milk and ice to bring them back. I knew that is what she would have done.

Like it or not, sometimes I had to bring some of them dope fiends back. Even at such a young age. To be honest, shit was far from being a joke back then.

Just another example of me being into some stuff, I had no business being in, or exposed to. In my defense, I did not put myself in that predicament, that was home for me. My reality, truth be told.

Chapter 5

My first boyfriend I met in Junior high school. I never forgot this story right here. Even though it happened such a long time ago.

I met this guy name Bug in the 7th grade. At first, I was playing hard to get. But with persistence, he eventually won me over.

He would walk me and pick me up from the bus stop every day. We began to deal with one another, and what not.

That is when I started cutting school going back to his sister's place/ where his family lived at. I started moving like I was grown, thinking I know something. Boy, was I wrong?

He had a whole lot of sisters. Some I am cool with to this day. His mother was such a sweet woman, God Bless her heart. A truly kind woman.

One of them special people you come across in life that makes you feel good. Basically, Good Vibes.

This is how this teenage love turned from sweet to sour very quickly. His mother fell on harsh times. We all knew that. That is why they lived with his older sister.

That was not even the problem. By then we were going steady. So, I thought nothing of what he was about to ask me for?

See my most recent birthday at the time, my mother had purchased me a nice size name plate with a nice size chain to match.

This was in the early 80's. So, you know what I am talking about if you around that time. That is when we were buying the real gold back then, I am just saying. I loved that chain.

With me feeling all in love, gullible and not knowing any better, I gave him my chain when he asked for it.

Then I noticed I did not see him for a couple of days. I figured maybe he was busy helping his mom and sisters. I found out later that he and his mother had moved to Rochester, NY.

Not only did I lose my boyfriend, but I also lost my birthday gift as well. Just like that I never saw him again. That was that bull shit, that was how I felt about it.

With my dad and this guy began my many reasons of why I have trust issues to this day. My name chain with the diamonds outlining my name and the Gucci link to match.

Come on! Out of all the things?

That still puzzles me to this day. My best friend in junior high school name was Solita. That was my partner right there.

Until she had to move back to her country. I think it had something to do with her papers. Immigration that is.

Later in life, I came across someone who was related to her told me the heart felt news about my friend.

Solita was murdered by her abusive boyfriend in her home country, St. Vincent. That right there, did not help my trust issues with men not one bit.

The ultimate reason for my trust issues of men came from the time I got raped. I had a dope body to match a beautiful face.

So, it was easy for me to get what I wanted out of men. I used what I got to my advantage. I met this Jamaican guy.

We used to go by his house and smoke up all his weed. He would give us money to get food. You know the munchies is for real.

He would always pull me to the side and mention that I should pay him a visit alone. Little did he know, I had no intentions of being with this guy alone.

That's the reason why I always came with my girlfriends. One night, nobody was able to go with me. My greedy ass decided to go alone.

My homegirl Bridget had to work at Mitchell's on Cornaga avenue. A very popular spot in Far rockaway. Everyone went there.

Zena couldn't go, she couldn't find a babysitter. Peannie was with her boyfriend. First, I'm going to blame myself for going alone.

I'm not blaming myself on what happened. I know I shouldn't have gone but wanting free weed had me on this mission of stupidity.

He gave me some weed. After that I was ready to go. I was about to leave. That's when he pulled out a gun on me.

He raped me. I couldn't believe this person raped me. I was upset, angry about it. I also knew I placed myself in that predicament.

I went to Mitchells afterwards. I fixed myself up. I washed my cat in the public bathroom at Mitchells. This was personal to me.

I only spoke about this to my current man and my publisher. Me getting this off my chest feels liberating at this point.

Chapter 6

While girls were playing double Dutch, dancing to their favorite music. Being a normal teenaged girl like the rest of them?

To be honest as possible, I am not the rest of them. I always remained in my own lane.

 By the age of 13, I was already smoking weed, drinking Quarts of Old Gold. Which was a nick name for Ole English beer.

Hanging out with my friends Angie, Kim and Theresa Green from around the way. Living like I was grown, not knowing this life I was experiencing was not normal.

But it was normal for me. It was all that I knew at the time. 14 years of age, I was selling Quarters of dope from my mother's project apartment.

In the Redfern housing project in Far rockaway Queens. Our apartment at the time was a drug spot.

Not only did we have products for sale. We also had designated spots within the apartment to shoot up, sniff, smoke.

Shit was like you buy the drugs in one room and get high in the next one. Sometimes with my mother.

Like I stated before, my mother was a functional dope fiend. Who was a great hustler? What is on momma's menu?

Everything is, that is on the menu? Dope, cocaine and anything else that you needed. We got it.

Everyone from my area knew my mother as Ms. Bobbie, the lady with the best dope in the rockaways at the time. Money was not a thing. Money was not ever a thing.

Not only did I learn the game from my mother first handed. Now comes into my life my second boyfriend, who name was Duke.

A well-known young person on the streets. He had an appetite for the game. Duke was a different kind of guy. He was just a money gamer.

Which meant he hustled for the money rush. Not for the means of support. He came from a middle-class family. Remember at the time technically we still were extremely young.

He did not need to sell drugs. But that was the choice he decided to make on his own. My young ass thinking I am grown and shit, respected that Shit.

We began, we became a couple before you knew it. We became closer and closer to the point of being inseparable.

I began to go on drug runs with him. He would buy his weight, his drug packages from a spot in Brooklyn. All that he was about at the time, I cannot front, it was a turn on to me.

The spot was on Liberty Avenue, in the East New York section of Brooklyn. That is where I met Virginia at.

She was a cool Puerto Rican woman. I met her a year before she got viciously murdered by a mad man.

She was part of the infamous Palm Sunday massacre. The Palm Sunday Massacre was the worst mass-murder in New York City at the time, to my knowledge.

Chapter 7

On a rainy spring evening was when the murders took place. Family members were sitting enjoying dinner while watching their favorite show on television.

Unknown to the family, a crazed individual broke into their home. They say the man was high out of his mind at the time. He enters with two handheld guns.

He ambushes these poor harmless people. All victims were shot in close distance.

Which made it a horrific scene, to say the least.

 The day, those murders happened will be known in history from that day forward. Will be known as The Palm Sunday Massacre.

Palm Sunday massacre was a 1984 mass murder homicide. That took place in the East New York section of Brooklyn. This resulted in the death of ten victims of circumstance.

The victims were three women, 1 teenaged girl, and six harmless children. All victims met their untimely demise. It happened around 5:30pm that dreadful evening.

To top it all off, one of the women found murdered was pregnant. The autopsy report stated the fact. The unidentified pregnant woman was in her 8th month of her pregnancy.

Ten lifeless bodies laid there at 1080 Liberty Avenue. The location of this Brooklyn address is located at the borderline of Brooklyn and Queens.

Most people in the area, refer to this area as City line. This is what the police discovered as they arrived on the scene.

There were no sign of drugs or robbery at the murder scene. But the police knew the house was owned by a well-known drug dealer.

Who by the way, was married to one of the murdered victims?

He was a heavy player in the drug game. He was already a convicted cocaine drug dealer. Well-known to the police department.

So, already you know the police officers felt a certain type of way about this situation. It was found out later, the assailant used two handheld guns in the murder.

He had a .22 caliber gun and a .38 revolver. A total of 19 bullets was shot that evening from those guns.

All members were of Hispanic descent. The bodies were discovered by a female relative hours after the crime took place. He found his dead relatives in the 1st floor apartment.

The apartment was part of a two-family house. The story goes the lunatic went room by room killing everyone in his path. Talk about an ambush?

Some of his victims were discovered with drinks and folks in their hands. This is what the detectives discovered upon arrival on the murder scene.

There was visible evidence that a slaughter had taken place. The path of destruction was left behind by this crazy individual.

Throughout the debris from the gun smoke, blood, dust and everything else. They discovered someone was still alive.

The lone survivor was a new-born baby. Seeing the new-born baby there in the crib made everyone in the room upset.

This sparked an absolute public outrage. This resulted in an all-out manhunt to apprehend this individual.

Once the story was on the evening news and in all the New York city newspapers the search expanded to a citywide search.

The investigation was headed by detectives from the 75th precinct, which is in East New York. All parties involved agreed that someone would have to pay for this heinous act.

What broke the case for the detectives was an anonymous call. The caller gave the detectives a name of a person who they believed committed the murders.

The name was given, became a name of interest. Pretty much, all they had at the time. To further the investigation the detectives had to get in contact with the husband of the deceased.

Interesting enough he said the same name that the anonymous caller gave. Now, the detectives knew they were on to something.

Now with a name it was all about placing a face, with the name. The detectives returned to the precinct. They wanted to look at the mugshot books. And check the name out.

They caught their suspect somewhere in the Bronx. He was arrested. In 1985, the assailant was convicted on ten counts of manslaughter.

To everyone's surprise when the verdict came back for murder? The jury chose not to convict him of any of the murder charges.

The reason given was he was high on crack, cocaine at the time of the murders. They said he was not in his right frame of mind.

The jury first convicted him on intentional murder. Later those charges were reduced due to emotional disturbance.

In other words, there is no love lost when it comes down to the family of drug dealers. Which regardless of the fact, this man murdered these people.

He was sentenced to, from 83 to 250 years in prison. Due to state law, he was expected to spend no more than 50 years in prison. In most cases, that would probably mean life.

Everybody thought they heard the last of this guy. Cut and dry, case over with. Lock him up and throw away the key.

Unfortunately, that was not the case. Then the unthinkable happened. After serving a couple of decades behind bars.

He was released around 2018. He served more than 32 years in prison. Many wanted him to get the death penalty. Most wanted him to at least spend the rest of his life in prison.

The law is the law, he maxed out on his bid. With good behavior, he was granted his freedom.

Of course, public outrage came behind that. Him being free, I felt that was bull shit. That is my opinion, and I am standing behind it.

Chapter 8

I remember it like it was yesterday. Going with Duke to re-up. The house he would take me to a drug spot, for weight. It was just more than that.

Maybe it started like that. But it surely did not end up like that. By us going there so frequently we began to build little friendship with the people involved.

One of the women I got really cool with. Her name was V. Whenever Duke and I would enter their 1st floor apartment we were greeted with love.

Little Junior would run up to me and give me a great big hug, every time he saw me. He had a little crush on me.

They would jokingly call little Junior my boyfriend. We would joke about this quite often. It was an icebreaker which all parties involved needed.

I would sit and watch T.V., basically hang out with the women of the house while Duke and the man of the house handle their transactions.

I would just chill and randomly have conversations with all the women in the house. Well, the ones who knew how to speak English.

Even the ones who did not know the language would wave at me and smile. Such a great group of people beyond what was taking place in the other room.

This was our routine. Duke would be doing what he was doing, and I would chill and wait. It was like clockwork.

V got pregnant. So, that became the conversation at the time. I would ask her when was she due? I liked her. I wanted to do something nice for her and her newborn baby.

Every time I saw her, I would ask her to have a baby shower. At the time, she told me she would have to get back to me with more information as it comes dealing with a baby shower.

The crazy part of it all, I knew where I was at. I also knew what we were doing there. Still this environment had a homely feel to it. At least whenever I was there.

I guess, you can call it mutual love. The real way to do business. It was way bigger than business, they treated Duke and I like family. I cannot front, I loved every part of it.

To put it in a better perspective everything was normal. Either I would go with Duke to the house in East New York. Or our re-up connection would me us in Far rockaway.

That last time was a couple of days before the Palm Sunday Massacre. He came to us in far rockaway to sell Duke a brick of cocaine. We met him in the McDonald parking lot on Mott Avenue.

As I reflect, look at life and the drug game. Even people who is not directly involved in the game can be affected by the game as well.

In life, you can be a pawn in this game that does not love anyone. It is a game that only takes, hurts, destroys and kills everything in its path. Look how life took an unexpected turn.

What was here today can be gone tomorrow. At this point, that was an understatement.

The people, the place was the same place and people who were murdered that dreaded evening on Palm Sunday.

See the connection. This took everything to a next level.

When the word hit the streets about who did this horrific act on these innocent people.

Even though the man of the house was involved with the drug game that does not mean his family was involved as well.

Come to find out one of my brothers used to sell weed for this certain person. We knew who it was. The question was, did anybody else know?

Chapter 9

It got real for me and Duke? When the Detectives began to question individuals.

All who had any type of dealings with the murdered victims or dealings with the well-known cocaine dealer, who they believed the hit was meant for.

Everything got hot when the Detectives interviewed his sister. She was not holding anything back.

She started telling the Detectives things they already knew about her brother. They wanted to know his business affiliates and who would want to kill her brother or his family.

She gave up many names, but no one knows what set of names she gave up to them. She knew numerous characters that he dealt with through the years.

Plus, that was her family too, if I am not mistaken one of her children was murdered that day too. So, I know she just wants justice. And I cannot blame her.

Now, the Detective had the spot list of names and numbers. It seemed like everyone who was connected to this guy was on the run.

Because everyone could not help but to think that the police was looking for them. To question them about these murders.

Duke and I had no choice but to go on the run like everyone else involved. Nobody wanted to get caught up in that shit.

The word was they was looking for everyone on his client list.

Duke was on that list for sure. While we were hiding out at my cousin Wendy's place. That was the plan until the smoke clears.

I knew, I knew the dirtbag who committed the murders. Then I remember more into detail what happened when one of my brothers sold weed for this guy.

Which did not end well. That led to an altercation with him and my brother. My brother ran off with the man's drug package.

Over that he sends threatening messages to get back to my brother. He was saying that he was going to kill my brother.

One of my other brothers stepped to him about the situation. That is as far as that went. We did not know at the time that he was built like that.

Capable of murdering somebody. Who would have ever thought, He got down like that?

After the Palm Sunday massacre Duke began to indulge more and more into drugs. Depression also played a part in it.

He was paranoid just about all the time at this point.

On top of that, he became abusive. Controlling, extremely jealous, it got so bad, I could not look in a man's direction without him having some type of feelings over it.

He really did not like me talking to people. It did not matter what it was about. He would tell me what clothes to wear, what friends I could have.

After a while, he only allowed me to have one friend. Only one homegirl I could hang out with. She lived in the building that was next to mine.

Come to find out, while he had me on lockdown, stuck in the house and everything.

He was out there tricking on coke with one of my mother's clients. Drugs for sexual favors was on the plate. Low down sneaky, shit.

After I found out what Duke was doing behind my back. In return, I started sleeping with the supplier.

Big Jay was the weight man. Who was old enough to be my father? That is when it began to get real. He was my mother's supplier too.

In this case, for my mom, this was a good thing. Because it avoided a lot of drama.

Drama behind her being reckless with the drugs. And with the drug money.

A bad thing because she would mess up packages regularly. I think she was doing that on purpose.

When she messes up a package, she used to try to send me with a made-up excuse to tell Jay.

What she did not know whenever she came up with her bull shit. I had my own personal stash.

Pretty much, all I had to do was walk to my closet and go get whatever she needed for the moment.

By me sleeping with Big Jay, all packages were right and exact all the time. I did not have to worry about that.

Back to Duke, I remember throughout all this madness I still had compassion for that man. So much when he went through his mental breakdown, I was there for him.

Even when they placed him in a mental institution. I remember when he was in Creedmoor Psychiatric Center. Which was located on the other side of Queens.

The point of enough was enough came in an unexpected way. I knew, I was done with him for good when I found out he slept with my nephew's mother.

I was not really sweating it like that. Anyways by then I was sleeping with the boss. So, it did not matter that much to me. I was hurt, but not ruined.

It seemed like as these experiences I went through added up. Where my maturity was ahead of my time really paid off. And was well needed.

Chapter 10

Big Jay was giving me so much dope to sell. If the police officers had decided to raid our apartment. My moms, and whoever else was in that apartment would have been in some serious trouble.

So much dope was there. It would have resulted in some serious prison time. Where they might have them locked up, to this day.

It still amazes me to this day how much dope we had in our place at any given time. Serious amounts of dope were moving daily.

With the different types of customers came through from so many races, so many different walks of life.

The only thing they had in common was addiction. See drugs don't discriminate. Now with providing the drugs, also came connections in all sorts of things and places.

For example, we had a dope fiend named Rose. Rose worked at the Sherwood diner. Which was located on the Rockaway turnpike.

She would come over with all types of meats and seafood to sell for some drugs. In return my mom kept a full deep freezer in the kitchen.

So many times, so many things we got from dope fiends. Too many unforgettable moments with those dope fiends.

Like the time Johnny the plumber stole some drugs in the apartment. Instead of him leaving with the stolen drugs.

My mother's girlfriend came over to pick up a package of work. My mother had left it out for her.

White boy Johnny comes over to buy and get high. He notices the package was there unattended. he quickly springs into action.

My mother's girlfriend name was Red. Red dealt with Sweet D... Talk about a ruthless couple. She was one of them chicks you really didn't want to mess with.

Johnny grabs the package of drugs. He places it where only he knew where to find it.

So, he thought. He places it in the bathroom somewhere around the toilet bowl. A place where only plumbers would know.

Instead of him leaving at this point. He decides to stay and hangout. Red couldn't find the package that was left for her.

She questions me, I tell her no one was here. The only person that came through was white boy Johnny.

In this drug game you must have a degree of intelligence. She remembers that Johnny was a plumber.

She checked around the bathroom. She found the drugs hidden behind the toilet bowl.

When we found out it was him who stole the drugs. He got his ass whipped. Red began to pistol whip this guy.

Yeah, Red kept a pistol on her. Sweet D made sure of that. Talk about someone mind being somewhere else.

Typical things we encountered that was part of the life of being in the drug game.

It was amazing how lives around the drug game could take so many different turns. Some turns for the worst. I don't believe in the gateway drug theory.

But some of my friends and I started smoking weed. Onto, smoking wooly blunts.

Some of them chicks graduated to the pipe. They went on to becoming full blown crack heads.

Those chicks would hang at the long island railroad train stop. It was the train's last stop.

They be out there prostituting to come up with money to buy drugs. It was crazy times. Some got into cars, and we never saw them again.

When the chick stole the jewelry out of the apartment. Some chicks came to my mother's place to hang out, buy drugs and get high.

It was this chick name Tee. Her sister Billy and their homegirl Jay. Jay didn't shoot dope. She sniffed coke. They would hang out with my mother.

My mother had over 17 chains. She would rock all her chains around her neck most of the time. She had a large jewelry collection.

My mother's jewelry was mostly bought from a white boy named Pete.

Pete would burglarize homes in the Cedarhurst and Woodmere areas in Long Island. Not too far from far rockaway.

Again, most of the time it was exchange for drugs. Rarely did my mom have to buy any of it with actual cash. In the drug game, the drugs were the cash.

When one of these chicks decided to steal our jewelry. With us not knowing at first. Then it was brought to my attention that some of our jewelry was missing.

Jay threw the jewelry she stole out of the window. This is what we learned later. But at that moment in time, I made all of them bitches' strip.

That shit got under my skin. I was prepared to whip all their asses if some answers weren't given. Because clearly the question at hand was, where the hells my mom's jewelry.

It escalated when my mother couldn't find her wedding ring. All my mother wanted back was her wedding band.

 She was like whoever took the jewelry could keep all the other stuff. Her main concern was her wedding ring.

That night them chicks couldn't come up with that. My mom told me to chill. She understood it was all part of the game.

For me personally, I did not understand that at all. Years later after the passing of my mother. I found out the true story of what took place that night.

I had stepped to the guilty chick about what had transpired. Make a long story short, she had to pay me money every first of the month when she got her check.

My mother was dead and gone by that point. Still that chick had to pay me. She paid me some money every first of the month until she passed away from aids years later.

For me it was personal. And when it's personal, it's personal. Too many stories and too many names to talk about at this moment.

Whenever my mother needed to re-up, she informs me to get in contact with Big Jay. Little did she know, I did not have to contact Big Jay.

I would pretend like I was though. Like I stated before, we had a large amount of dope in the apartment. My mother did not know that her stash was not the only one that was there.

I had a bigger stash of drugs in my closet than my mother. When she needed to get more. I gave her my drugs to sell.

She did not know it was my drugs she was selling. On the low, baby girl had her own operation going on.

Chapter 11

We knew Tee for a minute, everyone in the neighborhood knew who she was. She was another dope fiend that we grew close to.

Her and my mother got high together many times. Selling her body for drugs. Eventually she got caught up when she got pregnant.

During her pregnancy she remain living the way she was before. She went through a lot. She tried to get an abortion. But that did not work out for her.

She was high most of the time. Her mind was not thinking about that. Drugs will have your mind somewhere else.

Drug abused pregnant women covered these drugs infested areas throughout the country. My neighborhood was no different. Young strung on dope, lost, confused on so many levels.

She had the baby. Her baby was such a beautiful baby girl. It did not take any time at all for her to return to her old ways and habits.

While she was out scamming, and lord knows whatever else was out there to get drugs. She got in trouble shoplifting with her baby.

She got caught in one of the malls in Nassau County. She was arrested. She needed someone to get her baby.

So, she called the only person she knew, she could trust. Even though her and my mother shot dope together, my mother also took her under her wing.

You know like, she taught her a thing or two. She reached out to my mother to get her baby.

She knew, if my mother did not come, social services would of took her baby. My mom went and got her baby.

My mother had a big heart when came to things like that. Even though she had her own daily fight with her own personal demons. She had the compassion to help others in need.

Also, everyone wanted the baby to have a chance. From that day forward she was part of our family. Buttons was the nick name we gave her. Such a little, sweet baby girl.

Whenever people saw me with buttons, they always thought we were sisters. Sometimes, some thought we were mother and daughter.

I always carried myself more mature than my age. I also looked the part. We looked alike. I cannot deny that.

Everything was okay at first. She went from a healthy baby. We took great care of her. But as she started to grow into a little girl, she became ill.

She was sick all the time. When we took her to the doctor? He ran some test.

That is when we found out she was born with H.I.V. and by this time she had full blown out AIDS. She was one of the first cases reported. Which was a new disease at the time.

It was much research that was needed to be done with this new disease at the time. As she grew more ill, she was hospitalized. Where she had to remain there for the rest of her life.

They ran many test on her. They also studied her. They named the children's ward after her in one of the hospitals in Long Island.

She fought a good fight. Unfortunately, she died from the deadly disease. Buttons was seven years old at the time of her death.

Born under circumstances beyond her control. To be able to still make a giant impact in this world, is nothing less than amazing.

To me, that little girl will always be my champ. She will always have a place in my heart. We loved and cherished her. Word, Rest in Peace Buttons.

Chapter 12

So many sad stories blanketed constantly with the abundance amounts of money I made.

Having a big heart in this cold world has its ups and downs. I guess, it is all part of the game. Part of the life I chose to live at the time.

My mom remains selling dope for Big Jay. Now, Big Jay had a new partner, his name was Sweet Dee. This guy took real good care of us.

When he came into our operations, he took us to a whole next level. At the time. The only thing with him, he had this robbing bank fetish.

We were already making hell of money with the drug game. It is crazy to understand why would he want to do that?

I do not know what was going through this guy's mind. Like what was he thinking? Because during this whole time he was robbing chemical banks. It was all fun and games until he got caught.

When the story got out. We heard there were two masked gunmen who attempted to rob a Chemical bank, back in 1982.

The gunmen walk into the already crowded bank and pulls out their weapons.

A woman witnesses this from outside looking inside of the bank, through the glassed based entrance door. She begins to run away from the bank.

During the robbery two plainclothes policemen of the anticrime patrol was on their normal patrol.

Until they saw the terrified woman running away from the bank, she witnessed something unusual.

That caught their attention. It laid down rules for suspicion. So, they decided to check it out. The robbery was then interrupted by the plainclothes officers.

The bank was located on the corners of Mott Avenue and Smith place. Not too far away from the "A" train's historic Mott Avenue train station stop.

The officers carried their service revolvers beneath their civilian clothing. They went inside the bank to investigate what made the woman run away like that. This was a little before 10 am that morning, that day.

Upon entry they spot the gunmen. The gunmen were easy to spot. They were wielding their guns in the air.

Making demands to the bank tellers. They ordered the bank teller to place the money into a couple of large bags.

One officer went to get back up. The actual precinct was located a couple of blocks away from the bank. The police station was also located on Mott Avenue.

The remaining officer on the scene orders one of the gunmen to freeze and put down his weapon.

He also orders the bank employees and all the other civilians to drop to the floor. So, they could have instant protection from the estimated gun fire that was about to happen.

According to reliable sources one of the gunmen shouted to the other gunman to shoot the officer. By then, the officer retreats to find something to protect him from bullets.

The officer then fires five shots from his gun in the direction of the masked gunmen. As he shoots his service revolver he backs out of the bank's front door.

One of the bullets that was fired grazed one of the masked armed gunmen in the face. As the gunman advanced towards the officer.

After feeling the burn of being grazed in the face from a bullet, of a gun. Also knowing how close he could have gotten shot in the face.

He decided to surrender at that moment. Blood was gushing down the side of his face. He came outside of the bank and gave himself up peacefully.

Another bullet left a hole in the glass plated bank's entrance door. The injury the gunman received was not life threatening according to the police department.

That was discovered later when the police department made their official statement.

The second and remaining gunman fled up the stairwell in the bank during all the commotion. He came out of the stairwell on the second floor of the bank.

Where he found 4 employees and the bank manager. He quickly gathered them together. He held these 5 hostages.

Several bank employees and bank customers were able to escape safely with the help of the authorities.

They were escorted out of the bank's side door. Crowds of bystanders watched and witnessed this mayhem.

People watched from behind the police tape that was put up for everyone's safety. The standoff lasted nearly an hour.

The five remaining hostages and the lone gunman at this point, exited the bank one at a time.

The gunman was persuaded to turn himself in by a few negotiators of The New York City department hostage team. They were the ones who talked him into turning himself in.

All the money was recovered on the second floor of the bank. They also found three hand-held firearms. That was believed to be left by the assailants.

See many people thought I was messing around with Sweet Dee. But that was not the case. He would feel up on me, every once, in a while, but that was about it.

Especially, when I wore certain clothes in front of him. Before the untimely Chemical bank situation that derailed everything happened. I thought, I was on top of the world.

Which at the time, I did not think it was possible for me to come down? But after he got in trouble. Our lives changed yet again.

I got one of my friends to play hooky from school with me. We went to go visit him. Well, I tried to go visit. They shut me down when I arrived.

They told me and my friend was too young to visit inmates. Years went by, he kept in touch with me.

Eventually I wind up visiting him while he was in the prison called Sing-Sing. Something about that life always attracted me to it.

Chapter 13

My mother, out of all the people, decides to hook me up with someone she knows. Right there I should have known this was going to be a train wreck. I went along with it out of curiosity. I was around 17 years around this time.

What I saw? I was not expecting. He was a very handsome man. Dressed well, smelt good. He was an all-around attractive man. My eyes were pleased with what I was seeing.

We hooked up. And we got to know one another better. He would tell me, he worked for this diamond company in the diamond district in lower Manhattan, in New York City.

He always mentions to me, he was a very hard-working man. He was one of them dapper Dan type of men. He was always dressed in the latest. From his shoes on up.

Smelling good, jewelry looking nice on him. if he says he works hard for his money. Then whom am I to judge. He looked the part.

You know how they say, you work hard, you play even harder. His words were as good as gold to me.

Did I tell you how good that man looked? I am just being honest. The truth is the truth. We would go to Manhattan. He takes me to the diamond district.

Where we would go shopping for jewelry. Which is one of my favor things to do. He would show me all types of different jewels.

A girl could get use to this. This is the finer things in life. That I felt like I deserved. And of course, wanted.

It was like clockwork at the jewelry stores. I try it on. I wait outside.

In a couple of minutes, he comes outside with the necklace I tried on and then some. It was that simple.

Talk about a thrill, a head rush. I could not help but to feel like I was swimming in gold and diamonds.

We dressed up alike, we wore matching outfits. We would chill all over the city. He had it going on, on a next level.

We had things like, matching furs, minks and leathers. This was around the time when I started smoking joints, weed with sprinkles of cocaine covering it. Which on the streets was known as a wooly blunt?

Just when I was thinking shit was all good. What glitters is not always gold? Let me explain, how his shine was a mirage.

Sort of a figment of my imagination. His glitter was not gold. Not one bit, not one drop.

That is how that bubble got burst. When the truth came out this guy was a jewel thief. He was quite good at it.

If I do say so myself. That part right there really did not matter that much to me. I was used to dealing with individuals who most people would classify as criminals.

Hey, I got a thing for bad boys. I am not ashamed of that, either.

It was not the fact he was a thief. The problem was he was on dope. He was a dope fiend just like my mother.

My mother deceived me with that one. I remember getting high around my mother. Then eventually getting high with my mother. I would smoke my wooly blunt and she would smoke the shit, out of a pipe.

Chapter 14

I dated this guy named Homicide. On the streets he was known for being a livewire. He was so ruthless.

He was in an issue of the Jet magazine for spitting on a judge. A straight thoroughbred, heavily respected on the streets. His name rung bells.

He got out of jail. He wasted no time at all. He robbed a Jamaican weed spot. He came off with a couple of pounds of weed.

Plus, a nice amount of cash. That is how he did things around here. He takes what he wants. Most did not want any smoke from this fella.

He set up shop. He got me and my friend Shakema to sell a couple packages of weed for him. I already knew how to move packages.

That was not a hard thing for me to do. I knew, I did not have all the money. But I had a reason for not having it all.

I let him know upfront, I only had half of his money. Because the other half of the money I had invested it in buying and selling crack. Which tripled his profits.

Basically, I was flipping his drugs for him. He was pleased with that. Plus, he was turned on, by my street drug business knowledge.

He mentions, he did not know any girls who knew the drug game like that. I told him, well he met one. We just laughed and smiled at one another.

My hips and thighs and everything else occupied his mind. His eyes were all over me. I felt his energy.

Raw, uncut rugged energy he possessed. Especially, when I told him, I been sold his weed package. And all we were waiting on was the crack sales profits of the day.

Which in other words, The Money. I had to show him how fast I could flip the money and get it back with profit.

Only if you could of saw the look in his eyes. It is like he had a sparkle, almost teary eyed. Then he caught himself. You know he cannot look soft around me.

What I did read was he wanted to hem me up, wherever and do nasty things to me. His complete gesture showed it all.

At this point we both wanted to get closer to each other in more ways than one. Flames were burning desire, and it was a good feeling too.

Feelings had to be addressed. Desires had to be settled. What he wanted with me remained a mystery to me.

I knew he loved me. What extent I found that hard to describe. I believed he loved me a little too much. To where it became abusive.

It got abusive oddly, extremely quick. He started it out with being controlling. Then it went to him being a very jealous man.

When? I tried to confront him, about his ways and actions? He turned around and pistol whipped me. He gave me a serious beatdown that day.

He fought me a lot back then. Some of everything had me stay. I already had the understanding that he was a livewire. So, I kind of knew what to expect.

Our drug operation began to boom. After a while, I was able to buy my own package of crack. Not only were we lovers. We also became business partners at a point.

Money was pouring in so much. I was able to afford to have my own workers. With a livewire as a boyfriend, I did not have to worry about any drama, while I made my own moves.

He took it to another level when he began to think every man in the world wanted me. My body shape, my size and everything else was very appealing to men.

I was a piece of eye candy. And he hated the fact. What he did not understand was no matter what I did or wore men was going to notice me.

God created me like that, I could not help that part.

And If I could, why would I? God bless me with looks. Why would I be ungrateful about that.

Remember, millions of women would pay millions of dollars for a body like mine. My body curves were serious at the time.

His jealous thoughts became unbearable at times. He had the nerve to think one of my own brothers wanted me.

Which was crazy. The more he spoke and the more he carried on. I began to realize I was dealing with a psychopath.

All I could do at the time was shake my head in disbelief. As I did back then. I already had one boyfriend of mine go to the G building. Damn another one to the mental ward? Or how we say it in the hood, the nut house.

The day a crackhead came knocking on my door wanting to buy some crack. This man went crazy over it. He would not let me serve the customer.

 For what reason, I do not know? Because this was normal business. Like we always did. I really do not know what made that day any different from any other one.

Out of nowhere he begins to scream and yell at me. Then he went for his gun. He began to beat me with it.

As he kept on belting me with his gun, my girlfriend in the other room starts to scream.

She came into the room. She saw what was taking place. I told her to go get my mother and brothers.

Basically, I told her to get me some help. Since she was standing there all scared and shit. He turns around towards her.

He asked what did she want? What I thought she was going to say? Was not what she said.

Being in the drug game is for real. Constantly being around crackheads and dope fiends. Nobody to trust. Nobody to count on. Even with the littlest things.

Just having the basic understanding of knowing what is going on around you. Shakema asks him for 5. You heard right, all she wanted was 5.

I could not believe it, myself. He gave it to her. To get rid of her. And it worked. I knew then, I was in some serious shit.

I had to come to grips with what was at hand. Messing with this guy right now. I might not make it out of this place alive.

It got that real. And it got that intense. The beaten was not stopping. He just kept on hitting me and hitting me.

Totally overpowering me. I had to think quick. I had to think on my toes. I knew one way to defuse the situation. I was praying that it works. If it does not. Then I am going to have some serious issues.

I used what God gave me, my womanhood. I took off all my clothes and my jewelry. Laid in his bed in the nude.

I knew, I had to seduce him. My sexual advances he could not turn down. Especially when I started to do the thing he likes.

As I did what he liked. He could not help himself. He grabbed me and started to give it to me. We went at it for a long while. Until he was nice and tired. You know, relaxed.

As he laid there calm and relaxed. I told him, I needed to go to the store. And I was coming back.

He was good for the moment. He was not paying me any attention.

Clearly it was my time for me to make a move. I left out the apartment with the quickness.

When I got outside, the first thing I did was thank the Lord. God was the only way I was getting out of that place alive. I must acknowledge that.

I left just about everything upstairs. My clothes, my jewelry, etc., up there. But I was not trying to go back up there to get anything.

That was not going to happen. I loved and valued my life a little too much. To be up here gambling it all away over things I could always replace. I had a serious gut feeling things were not going to end well.

I could just feel it. A few minutes went by, and I see my friend who left me upstairs getting my brains bashed in. She looked at me and smiled.

By the look on her face. She did not do anything I ask her to do. She did not get my mother nor my brothers.

She sat there, scared. I could not even be mad at her. For me, things been way out of hand. Way out of control.

Things got so bad. The way I was feeling. I just knew I had to get away for some time. I was up to my head in emotions.

Shit had me so paranoid. I went into hiding. I felt that was the best move for my safety. I did not know what to expect when it came down to my boyfriend at the time.

I stayed by my girlfriend Winnie's place. She lived in Wave Crest a small complex off Segrit Blvd. and Beach 20th St., up the block from the beach.

Chapter 15

I had heard there was going to be a big event at the club. They told me who party it was, but I cannot recall exactly who told me. Or, who party it was?

All I knew at the time, I was bored, locked away at a friend's place. I wanted and needed to get out.

I wanted to go and have some fun. Everyone was going. Including my brothers. I knew I did not have too much to worry about.

So, I decided to go. I went to have myself a good time. The plans were short, sweet to the point. When I got there the place was jamming.

I just knew this was going to be an incredibly good night. Music was good. Overall good vibes. Everything was all good.

Finally, I got to unwind relax, chill and have a good time. I did not have to worry about looking over my shoulder. I could enjoy myself.

Now, I am at the bar. Music is jumping. I am dancing, moving my hips from side to side as I sip on my drink. Bopping my head every now and again.

The energy at Club Hollywood was magnificent. The DJ was playing my jams all night long. I was so happy that I went. I was getting tempted to get on the dance floor.

That was how I was feeling. My drink, I was drinking was everything too. Back in Far Rockaway, someone who was not minding their own business tell RJ where I was at?

He asked a random person, who we both know about my whereabouts? They tell him exactly where I was at. Why would somebody do that?

Now, this crazed individual decides to go to the club. He walks inside the club solely looking for me. He asks a couple of people about my whereabouts in this club.

A random individual spotted me for him. Once his friend noticed me, he points in my direction.

The bad part about that, was his friend pointed at me while I had my back turned. So, I was completely unaware this guy was looking for me. Or he was in the same club I was in.

Talk about an awkward moment. I was moving my hips side to side, sipping on my drink. I was enjoying the music and my drink.

Rocking without any cares in the world. While this man watches me from a far. Not even knowing he is in this club.

I was dancing with my back towards the crowd. I did not want any attention. I was not looking for anybody.

Honestly, I did not want nobody. I had enough issues and problems with the "so-called" man I already had.

When he tapped me on my shoulder, I was caught off guard. I was not expecting this to happened. I went from chilling, at ease, having a good time.

To feeling unjust, uneasy, all jammed up. A feeling I did not want to have. A feeling I just wanted to go away.

I turned towards him when he grabs my arm. He wanted me to go home with him. I knew what that meant. If I go with him. I knew he was going to kill me.

All the signs were there. It was clear as day. At this point, I would be a fool to leave this club with this man. As uneased as I felt. I was surely glad we were in a public place.

This crowded club was God send at the time. Lucky for me people was everywhere in this jammed pack club.

That made me feel a little safe. Because this nut would pop-off anywhere.

Dealing with a livewire type of hoodlum. These types of men are liable to make disturbance anywhere, at any time. They did not care.

Especially my boyfriend, he was made without an off switch. Talk about 0 to 100 in a matter of second.

Unapologetic rough neck. The look in his eyes said all. I started to look around the club. I needed to see somebody I knew.

I saw my brothers. I did not know if he knew that. It was time for me figure out how to get out of this shit.

I went to the lady's room. I needed a moment to get myself together. I used the bathroom.

After I washed my hands, I looked in the mirror to fix my hair. As I stare into the mirror, I could not help but notice the hurt and embarrassment that came along with it.

Maybe the way I looked could hide my true expression. But my eyes could not hide the pain of being in this predicament.

I took as much time as possible in the bathroom. After I exited the lady's room. I saw one of my brothers. I was not that far away from where I was standing.

I walked up to him. I tell him the deal. He thought nothing about how I was feeling. He thought I was drunk in my feelings.

Plus, he knew how me, and my boyfriend always went back and forth. Beefing one day. Loving each other the next.

He did not know about any of the extra stuff me and RJ was going through. I kept my love life private from my brothers.

My brother looked into my eyes. Then he knew and felt something was not right with me.

I know for a fact, because my facial expressions were not hiding anything now. He could tell I was scared off my body language.

Still, he could not call it. He was concerned. Little did he know at the time. My boyfriend and I was absolutely going through something.

The little something my brother did not know about my relationship with this guy was it was as real, as real gets.

When I mentioned to brother, my boyfriend wanted me to go back to his place with him. His response was why was I telling him this?

I stated to my brother I was scared. He offers to go with me. If that was going to make me feel any better.

Both my brothers suggested they go with me and my boyfriend back to my boyfriend's place. I understood what they were trying to do.

But they did not understand what we would be getting ourselves into by accompanying this madman.

I knew deep, down inside something was not feeling right. I had a gut feeling about that one. Most of the time when this happens, something happens?

I went to look for my boyfriend. I could not find him. But I knew he was somewhere around, watching me look for him. Which I thought was totally crazy.

I just got myself prepared to leave the club with my brothers. I really did not have to worry about him. Trust and believe he will find me when he needs and wants to.

I walked out of the club. RJ watches me from a distance. He was obsessed with drama.

It was like he wanted something to go down. He wanted something to unfold, something to happen.

Thinking things into existence both negative and positive sometimes does not equate to what you really ask for. Because many times what you ask for is what you get.

I began to walk out of the club to get to the street. I walked pass a group of guys who were standing next to the entrance of the club.

One of the fellows touch me on my waist to get my attention. I quickly turned around to see who was touching me like that.

When I looked in the direction where the touch came from. A guy told me about a message from another guy who was also outside in front of the club.

He tells me some guy wanted to talk to me. He was just the messenger. Since this guy wanted to be the messenger, I told him to tell whoever gave him the message that I was not interested.

He was not trying to get with me, himself. Out of all these years that went by. I wanted to mention that. Because to this day I wondered why did he do that?

My crazy boyfriend looked and observed from a far. He stood there going off his own vision.

With his own crazy thoughts. That he created in his own mind. And people's body movements. He watched enraged. Jealousy filled up his body from his own ignorance.

Chapter 16

After what he thought he saw from a far. He sprang into action. He confronted the guy over what he thought was going on.

 He rushes the guy. The guy runs back into the club. He follows in pursued. They began fighting on the dance floor.

Which abruptly stopped the music. People began to yell, scream and panic. My boyfriend was seriously beating down this random guy in a jammed packed club.

As the fight got wilder and wilder, more fights begin to break out. Now a great amount of people was fighting one another.

My brother tries to defuse the situation by getting the Jamaicans outside of the club. And kept the black Americans inside.

In hindsight, it was not a smart move to make. It was a great side of relief, a temporary fix. To say the least. Still, I did not think it was the right move.

While we were trapped off in the club. Remember they pushed the Jamaicans outside of the club?

Since they were already outside. They had easy access to their weapons which were hidden in their cars.

Which resulted in us being at a serious disadvantage. Back then we had no cell phones to call for back up.

Nobody was going to call the police. Street rules applied in this situation. Eventually we would have to leave the club. Everyone knew this who were involved.

We also knew they were waiting for us outside. We were able to see that looking out the window. A small window.

I walked outside the club with my boyfriend walking behind me. This was surreal to me.

The same man who wanted to kill me initially. Who to my knowledge still wanted to? My thoughts were now this is some serious shit, For real, though.

As I walk outside of the club all I heard were gun shots. Right there, I cannot lie, I must have had an angel standing next to me. Protecting me.

Because I felt the warmness of a bullet as it passed my face. In extreme close range. The missed bullet missed me. But the bullet struck RJ in the chest.

He dropped and I ran to hide under a car. I was scared, shocked with all types of emotions flowing through my body. It is hard for me to grasp into words on how I was feeling at the time.

Crowds of people, just about everyone was screaming and yelling. Throughout the noise and chaos, I could hear my brother tell RJ to hang in there, to stay awake, and do not go to sleep on him.

Tears ran down my chubby cheeked face. Feeling helpless under a car during this mayhem.

My family and friends were trying to locate me. My brother began to scream my name to see where I was at.

Mainly to see if I was all right. I came from beneath the parked car I was hiding under. I caught eye contact with my brother. He saw me and he looked down.

Then he moved away so I could get a better look. I saw my boyfriend's lifeless body lying there on the concrete pavement.

I froze for a moment. One thing I knew for a fact, I knew his feelings for me. I knew he loved me.

I felt crushed. This turned into one of the worst days and feelings in my life. Like I said, one of them.

I had plenty of my share. One thing I knew was you cannot explain the unexplainable. And it makes no sense trying to figure it out either.

For example, my boyfriend wanted to kill me. In the process he winds up dead. Puzzling thoughts wrapped my mind.

I had to come to grips that it had to be a higher power than myself that protected me.

Seriously my back was against the wall with no way of getting out. And just like that I was freed. I had a lot to be thankful for. Starting with my life.

After the passing of RJ, all things I left over there where he lived at. This when yet again this took another route. This time over my belongings.

When it got weird to me. It was not even three after the killing of her son.

At this point she already did something with my things. Because every time I asked her about my belongings, it was always an excuse. Excuse after excuse from this lady is all I heard.

My assumption of it was my clothes and jewelry were not there anymore. If they were?

I would not be getting the run around over it. I think I just wanted them to be honest about that.

I really did not have the time nor desire to worry about materialistic things. Problems just kept on mounting up.

I lost my brother David. He got murdered. He was killed in a domestic altercation.

Even though we his family felt like we did not get justice over his killing. We remained sure of what really happened to my brother.

The family's feelings on it were they felt it was very foul thing that happened to him.

Chapter 17

After all that has happened. I needed a break, I needed to get away. When my sister reached out to me to help watch her kids while she made her money to support her, by stripping in the strip club.

I was with it. It was a no-brainer to me. At this point a change of scenery is what I absolutely needed and wanted.

I traveled to Baltimore, Maryland. While I was there, I started to watch the money flow of a stripper. I realized it was a lot of money to be made in the strip club game.

Another game in this game of hustling. Once I learned the ends and outs of the stripper game.

I decided to go back to New York and recruit a couple of strippers for my stripper racket.

At this point I already had the connection through my sister at the strip club. Now I had a couple of strippers working there.

I literally was transporting these chicks from New York to Baltimore, back and forth. Money was being made. Honestly that was my main concern.

In Baltimore my youngest brother was getting money doing the drug thing. He had set up shop selling crack outside/inside the stripper joint.

I was holding 90 8-balls of crack in a knap sack for my brother Baby Don. After we sold out. My sister got us a ride back to the hotel we were staying at.

When my sister pulled up with her ride. A man named AZ was driving her. We had just sold some of what we had to a couple of hoes who worked at the club. We got in the car with my sister and one of her clients.

She said, AZ was from Brooklyn. As we rode in route to the hotel. A random conversation turned into a heated exchange of words. One thing for sure everyone in the car was riding dirty.

The conversation took a turn when it was stated who was making the most money. Her friend was out there hustling too.

It got so intense he eventually kicked us out of his car. I guess, my brother got into the guy's feelings. Him kicking us out of his vehicle was a good thing for us.

One of them slick chicks at the club was trying to set us up with the police. Unknown to all the parties involved my brother and I had already exited the vehicle we left the strip club in.

See, me and my brother took a cab the rest of the way back to the hotel. We were in the clear.

What we found out later, my sister told us a couple of blocks after they dropped us off, more like kicked us out of the car.

The police officers pulled them over. They busted her and her client, AZ. The officers found a single $20 bag of crack in the vehicle.

As they searched the guy's car. Which was nothing compared to how much drugs the guy sold out of his car.

They were arrested on the spot. My sister and the guy got out the following day. Yet again, I got away unfazed, unscratched, most important untouched.

Chapter 18

After my little stint in Baltimore, Maryland. I came back to Far Rockaway, back to the Redfern housing projects.

Before you knew it, I was back on the block hustling. Doing what I do. Doing what I was good at.

As I do what I do, one day a limousine pulled up on me and my crew. At first, we

didn't know what to think about that.
Then the limousine drove away.

A few days later, the same limousine was back on our strip. The limousine pulled up right in front of us. The back window rolled down. The guy asked to buy 10 twenties of crack.

I only had 5 twenties of crack on me. At the time of the sale, I gave the gentlemen what I had.

I explained to him I was going upstairs to get the rest of his order together. Also, to get more work to sell.

He gave me $200 for 10 twenties of crack. By the time I got back downstairs and out of my building the limousine was gone. I guess, the white guy thought I was trying to rob him and take his money.

I was a little mixed up about that. I might do a lot of things foul. But beating someone out of their money just wasn't my cup of Tea.

I honestly felt a way about it. Hopefully he will come back. I hate feeling like I owe someone money or anything else.

About a week later, I came across the same man again. He came straight to me to buy crack.

I gave him what he paid for. And what I owed him. Plus, a little bit more for being a good sport about the mishap.

Since then, we had hit it off. We became buddies, partners, pals, etc. It got to a point where he could call whenever he felt. The time nor the day mattered, when it came down to this client.

If he wanted to purchase some crack for me? I was more than willing to accommodate his wishes. I would bring the product to him. Or I would send someone with the package to deliver it for me.

It was like clockwork, He call, we deliver. More like he is buying. And we are selling. Money being made. You know that's my type of party. It was that simple.

He would pay me a hundred to $200 to deliver the drugs to him. Then he would buy all the drugs I had on me.

Since his drug habit was heavy. I was over by his house frequently. We became great friends.

I was there so much I would help him clean up his big house. I would sleepover on some occasions.

I eventually met his mother and his sister Cookie. We used to barbecue in his massive size backyard.

We partied all the time. When we went out to eat. He would take us to Atlantic beach, in Long Island.

The lobsters he would buy was as big as newborn babies. The lobsters were huge for real. So, you know that is not cheap.

The lobsters were fresh, nice and juicy. He always went out in style.

Being around Italian Danny, I began to be around his circle of friends. I would provide cleaning services for those people with the real money, in the process.

Everything was set up perfect. With perfection comes a catch, just like everything else that has transpired in my life thus far.

His mom's such a sweet woman. They had no business messing with her. God bless her heart.

Chapter 19

Stack Bundles my beloved nephew. I love all my nieces and nephews dearly. They are like my kids I didn't have.

Back in the days my brother, his girlfriend and I used to rap. Back when hip-hop was a new thing.

Back when hip-hop was not being recorded. Most hip-hop you had to witness in person. Most of it was live.

Our names were Cool Rae Cee, Classy E and I was Delicious Dee. They were in a group called Soul Control.

Honestly, I was a more of a want to be down with what they were doing.

My other brother was a dancer. He was extremely good at it. He was well versed in all types of different music genres.

He was known to many as Disco Dave. My nephew got his dancing skills from my brother for sure.

My nephew Ray was on the showtime at the Apollo amateur night with a group of dancers from far rockaway. He always loved to perform. It was in his nature.

My brother and his girlfriend were Rayquon Stack Bundles Elliott's parents. My brother Raymond and Yvette Almira Elliot.

His parents were rapping in the early days of hip-hop. None of us in the family were surprised when he chose to rap for living.

My brother Stacks rap style was wicked. That's where my nephew got his rap name from. My nephew and I were very close.

He was raised by his Aunt Mazzini. She raised him while my brother was out of town locked up. And his mother was on drugs.

His first love was dancing. But when he got older, and he found his true calling it was a wrap after that. That is when my nephew took it to a whole next level.

I used to tell him always to watch himself. I wanted him to be safe. He would respond to that with Auntie I like to keep my enemies close.

Then we both laugh. Because that was just my nephew being a smart ass. I loved that boy.

He went to the movies to see 50 cent's new movie at the time, get rich or die trying.

While in the movie theater some guys tried to run up on him. Some beef from way back when.

50 cent was there as well viewing the movie. When the commotion went down. 50- cent, sent his bodyguards to handle it. They help my nephew get away that day.

Later, when I saw him, I told him he needs to relocate. Jealousy, envy and hate is very powerful.

We both knew at this point; he was a target for all the above. He agreed. But at the time he kept putting it off.

 I was trying to explain to my nephew that he needed to get off these streets. I was stressing the fact that he had a bright future in the entertainment industry.

He asked me to help him find a place. I told him I'll see what I can do.

That brought a smile to his face. In a matter of two weeks after the last time I saw him, my nephew Stack Bundles was murdered. He was found there with a bag of white castles on the ground next to him.

The reports were that he was on his way home coming from white castle. He had gone to get something to eat. What got me, was my nephew died on an empty stomach.

I remembered, I had to be strong, because I had to speak to the media on my family's behalf. Such a wonderful person gone too soon.

Rest In Peace nephew, Rayquon Maurice Elliot aka "Stack Bundles"

Chapter 20

My mother had so many so-called friends. People use to come and cop dope. Babysitter or not was going to stop an addict from getting high.

They bring their kids with them. Our Livingroom would be packed full of children on any given day.

That's why till this day, I have many fake cousins. Those kids would be at our house so much. They became family.

It almost became a job. In some cases, it was a job. I had to watch these kids. I had to cook for some of these kids. I had to do a little of everything.

In many situations when a parent is on drugs, which lead to many cases of child neglect. These kids came from all different walks of life.

Different backgrounds, different colors. Black, white, Spanish, it really didn't make a difference.

All these children sat in our Livingroom while their mommy, some cases their daddy was in the other room, behind a lock door getting high shooting dope with my mother.

Around the 1st of the month and the 15th of the month our house would be jammed packed. Some kids were at our house for days at a time. Because their mom when on a drug binge.

Or chicks would be on missions, and nobody knew where they were for a couple of days. Drug doesn't discriminate, drug addiction knows no color.

One of the kids that was in this predicament always thought he could rush his mother.

At first, he could not comprehend what was really going on with his mom.

It was crazy, unfortunately we all could relate. I know, I could.

Eventually he got angry, but at least he knew what time it was from then on. At that point, she wasn't fooling anybody anymore.

He still didn't want to play with the other kids. He just wanted his mother out of that room.

He used to talk to her through the door. He threatens his mother by saying he was going to tell his grandmother on her.

All he knew was his grandmother lived in the building next to ours. Being around all these kids and me being one as well, just a little older. We all had something in common.

Our mothers were addicts.

Watching these kids turned to me caring for these kids. Looking out for people who couldn't look out for themselves.

That's why I never wanted to have children of my own. Maybe because I experienced so much bull shit as a child myself. Also, I clearly saw firsthand how screwed up this world is.

I just never wanted to be a baby mama. When a relationship is over for me, I didn't want any reasons for a man to have to come back.

So, when I got pregnant at 16 years old from Duke. I stole my mother's Medicaid card and me and my friend Dena went to Mott Avenue abortion clinic.

I got rid of twins. I was not having no kids. I already had to take care of my siblings and the other drug addicts' children. That was enough for me.

I felt like talking about it because people thought I couldn't have children. I just never wanted any.

Directly or indirectly, taking care of people became a part of my life. It will continue to play a part as well.

My childhood experiences would be one sign on what's to come.

Another sign was when my mother was dying from AIDS, the way them home health aides treated her was not to my liking.

I told my mother how I felt about it. She tells me, I would do a better job than these so-called home health aides. Then she stated I should be one.

She explains to me why she thought that. She told me to show them how it's supposed to be done.

Later, I went and became a certified home health aide. That job saved my life at the time.

I always had a caring, loving heart. Taking care of people was no problem for me. It was like second nature.

I always cared and believed God had my back all a long throughout my life. My beloved clients Gema, Sal, and Doris. I gave my patients lots of love.

When you cared about people from the heart. A job like that becomes secondary. When I first met them, they all thought I was crazy.

They weren't used to someone showing love the way I do. Most of them home health aide was there for the money.

Once they realized I wasn't there for that. I was there to assist them with life. With sprinkling love on top.

I was 28 when I became a Home- health aide. Which was a complete game changer for me.

Chapter 21

I had my friend from the hill in Brownsville take me uptown to Harlem to purchase 10 grams.

 It was 20 dollars a gram of crack. I had 200 dollars at the time to play with. The spot was on 151st street and Broadway in Harlem.

I had on my jewelry. Plus, Lil Donny let me wear his big chain. Lil Donny wanted to come upstairs with me to the spot.

But I told him to chill, I got this. His father was a Brooklyn drug kingpin. I didn't want my homeboy to be all in my business like that. It was nothing personal.

My homeboy was on parole at the time anyway. I really didn't want my friend to get into any kind of trouble.

Lucky for him, when I got upstairs the spot got raided. I was caught up in a sting operation. It was one of the biggest drugs bust in Harlem at the time.

It was a Dominican spot. When you arrive at the building crackheads run up to you. They escort you to your destination.

This operation the Dominicans had was different to say the least. They paid their crackheads to bring their weight clients to them.

Inside of the building I was greeted by a black guy and a Spanish chick. They began to argue over who was going to receive the credit for walking me to the door.

When they opened the door, they asked me who brought me upstairs?

I really was not paying attention like that. I told them that they both brought me here.

The guy closes the door on the crackheads as they continued to argue over who brought me there.

I normally dealt with the spot on a lower level of the building. This time I was on a different floor in the building.

I was at a spot I never been before. They first checked me. They wanted to make sure I wasn't the police.

I heard a big commotion coming from outside of the door. It was coming from the hallway.

I figured it was the crackhead man and woman still arguing over who was going to get the credit for bringing me.

Nope, it was not the crackheads arguing. Instead, it was TNT, which stands for Tactical Narcotics Team.

The TNT squad raided the building. When the police knocked on the apartment door where I was in.

The Dominicans had pulled their guns on me. Like I was police or something. Then I told them, I was in just as much trouble as them. Everyone was on their own when the police knocked down the apartment door.

At this point everything was moving in slow motion at a fast pace. As the door went down, I made a break for the window.

I figured I'd jump out of the window. Shit, I'll do anything to get away at this point.

I pulled up the window. I looked outside and down. I saw a crowd of police officers and TNT looking up at me as I looked down on them.

A female police officer instructed me to come downstairs. I placed my leg back into the apartment, from the fire escape.

I laid my behind down facing the floor waiting for the police to come get me.

I absorbed all my options. The door to the actual room me and the Dominicans were in, was bolted shut. Once the police officers raided the front door of the apartment.

Everyone ran to the room that was bolted. They had so many locks on that door. It took the police a little while to get that door open.

We had extra time to run. But we had nowhere to go. They had the whole building surrounded.

One of the Dominicans shitted on himself, that was how afraid he was of the unknown. They placed me in handcuffs.

As the police officers escorted me out of the building, I saw Lil Donny talking to the police. They allowed him to come over to me and to take the jewelry off me.

It was news reporters, cameras everywhere. Just about everyone, everywhere were police. They were so many undercover officers on the scene.

That just showed me they had this operation under surveillance. Just the way they approached this raid.

From an ice-cream truck, construction workers, just so many undercovers. There were two apartment buildings connected to one another. Both building had numerous drug spots in them.

When I got to the precinct, they tried to charge me with being part of the Dominican crew I got arrested with.

I shut that down when I told them I was there just to buy some crack.

At first, they didn't believe me. Because of the way I was dressed. Lil Donny told my aunt what had happened to me.

Everybody in Redfern projects already knew what happened. All they had to do was turn on the evening news.

They had me walking out of the building in hand cuffs on the evening news. On all the three major New York television stations.

Lucky for me, the charges got dismissed. I had to stay on Riker's Island for a week. While my short time on Riker's Island I met a male correction officer.

He became my boyfriend. The crazy part of it all, I didn't even use my name. I used my sister's name during the ordeal.

Chapter 22

My brother Sport came home from doing 4 years in green correctional facility. I held him down his whole bid.

Since I had no kids, I was able to accommodate him more. I could go and visit him more often.

He was even paroled to my house. One day he told me he'll be back. He had this look in his eyes. This look didn't sit well with me.

But I didn't want to stress my brother out, sounding like I was a parole officer. Asking him where he was going. The last thing he needed was stress, or someone attempting to stress him out.

I remember when my boyfriend and I, at the time Danny got into a real heated confrontation. Which resulted in my brother kicking Danny out of my place.

He told him not to come back. When he saw Danny back in my place the next day. You could tell he had so much to say. But he kept it to himself.

My brother had let me know he was going to the store. I went to my lawyer's office.

while I was there taking care of business. I got a disturbing phone call.

My brother Nuke informed me someone gave our brother a bad bag of Dope. We heard that he was in Gino's pizzeria on Beach 20th street.

A half a block away from Mott Avenue. A very famous pizza spot in the Far rockaway section.

He ordered two slices of pizza. He went into the bathroom to shoot up some dope. He died of a drug overdose.

Deep down inside I always felt it was my mother's fault by exposing me and my siblings to drugs and all that came with it.

That killed me inside. I was down and out over this one. Danny reassured me that he was going to be there for me.

He told me not to worry about it. He comforted me by saying everything will be all right. Plus, time heals everything.

Chapter 23

The next month Danny tells me he's going upstate New York. He explains his reasons for taking the trip. He was traveling to Schenectady, a town in New York state.

Before he went out the door, I told him not to go. He was already on the run from the feds. I really wanted him to turn himself in. I wanted him to get it all over with.

I knew why he was taking the trip. I didn't like the fact he was going up there to help someone else with their beef.

I felt like that was that man's fight, not his. But you know how guys are, they are loyal to their street teams. Which to me, sometimes it's not fair to them.

No matter what I said. He wasn't trying to hear any of it. His mind was already made up. All I can do at that point was to tell my man to be safe. I couldn't help but to worry.

We were speaking periodically on the phone during his trip up there. Also, while he was there. I was planning a barbeque for him when he got home.

First, we lost phone communication. The last thing he told me he was on his way home.

They just had to handle one more thing. I called and he stop answering his phone. Which I found to be extremely odd, even for him.

But I didn't want to jump to any conclusions. So, I just let it play out. I figured I see how this all goes down.

Time started passing quickly, it seems like minutes turned into hours. Still, I haven't heard a word from him.

I started to think that maybe his phone was dead. And probably I was over thinking it. I do, do that quite often. I cannot lie.

I was devastated when I got the called that he has been murdered. Somebody shot and killed him. I was completely crushed.

Now, I was tired of losing people that I love. I felt so deep into a depression I wanted to die. But I wasn't going to kill myself. Because I had a relationship with God.

Honestly, I was praying that hopefully I could get hit by a Mack truck. Something of that nature to come and take me up outer here. Because the Lord knows at that time, I felt like I had nothing to live for.

Chapter 24

I just wanted something to ease the pain. It was unbearable. Very hurtful losing my brother one month and losing my man the next. It was a double whammy.

I laid there on my couch day in and day out. I just cried and prayed. I sat there isolated from the world. My God sister Kay would come and check on me.

She knew I was going through it. And she was there to help. She came by every day after work, to check on me.

My cousin Linda wanted to come and stay with me. I remembered a couple of months before his passing he had kicked my cousin out of our place.

I decided that I'll let her stay. But then I felt awkward about the whole thing. I knew that's not what Danny would've wanted.

I just wasn't feeling it. Or maybe it was too soon. But I wind up telling my cousin she had to bounce.

It wasn't personal, it was what he wanted. I wanted to pay and show him respect. At least I could do that for him.

My God sister would speak to her man everyday while she sat with me. I was losing so much weight. My God sister made sure I ate.

She kept on telling me about the guy she was dealing with. His name was Born Unique. Every time she mentions me to him.

He would always tell her that he knew me. But when she asks me about him. I didn't know any dudes by that name.

Then finally we were able to put one and one together. I ask her what his real name was.

Still his name didn't resonate with me. Until she said Little John. That's when I knew exactly who she was talking about.

Little John was a guy I went to junior high school with. He was one of my childhood friends. I know they were trying to help me get out of my depression.

My homegirl Nicky came over. She was trying to get me to go out. She was trying her best to get me off my couch.

She finally persuaded me to get some fresh air. But that didn't work.

I stayed on the couch all day and all night. I didn't want to sleep in my bed no more. Because Danny wasn't there.

Shit like that would have just reminded me of him. And my feelings would get hurt all over again. I told Kay did she know any nice guys where Little John was at.

At this point, I just wanted someone I could talk to. Little John mentions his cellmate. Little John called me to tell me he passed my number to his cellmate.

He was giving me the heads up, that his cellmate is going to call me.

Then I had a change of heart. I told little John, no. I didn't want to talk to the guy. I wanted to wait until I die, so I could be with Danny again. Even I knew that was unrealistic.

So, here I was falling deeply into my own depression. A couple of weeks later, God gave me the strength to get out of my depression. I send the word through my God sister to tell the guy to call me.

He called me, my first thoughts were maybe he just wanted to use me for packages and shit. Clearly, he had to been aware I was in a depression.

I thought he just wanted tuna fish, sneakers and fruit packages. When he called, I mention tuna and packages. He informs me he couldn't receive any of the stuff, I mentioned to him.

He reminded me that he was in the Feds. Things work differently in the Feds. Federal penitentiary is a whole different ball game. I told him; he was my kind of inmate.

He started calling me for about 4 months. After that I went to pay him a visit. We connected, I started visiting him regularly. He was locked up with Michael Douglas's son.

I was a huge fan of his work. I used to sit and talk to Mr. Douglas until Rich came out. Rich would come out and move us to other seats in the visiting room.

Rich would call me a groupie over this one. Every now and again I would sneak to talk to Mike before Rich came out.

On the other side of the Federal penitentiary housed one of the chicks from Housewives of New Jersey.

Rich was released after serving 12 years in the Feds. I did the last 6 years with him during his stretch. Rich was the most inspiring and motivational man I have ever dealt with.

Even while he was incarcerated, he still was able to lead me in the right direction. To me, my man is simply amazing. He pushed me to go ahead and get my nail salon licensing.

With the proper licensing I was able to open my nail salon. I became the first and only black owned nail salon in far rockaway.

With the right motivation, you'll be amazed on what you can do. I had my driver's learners permit for 35 years.

Rich had me go out there and finally get my driver's license. Not only that, now I'm finishing up on getting my real estate license.

When people say that people in jail is only looking for packages. I'll be the first one to disagree on that one. Because the one I got, damn sure made me a better person in the long run.

Rich came home and ask me to be his wife. Now I'm planning my big wedding.

Home health aide saved my life. I never sold drugs after that. I changed my life for the better. What don't kill me makes me stronger.

I would like to Thank you Jullian Smallwood for writing and publishing my book. I could have not done it without you. You are so amazing and intelligent to me.

I can't thank you enough because this is something I just needed to do. I pray some young girls out there can learn from my experiences and mistakes.

I also want to send a special thanks to my friend for decades, Janel Hawthorne for introducing Jullian to me. I tried meeting him for a long time.

One more thing, a special thanks to my Fiancé Richard Crawford.

My attorney the best in the world: Anthony Mallilo. My doctors, Dr. Ann Bule and Dr. Lewis Marshal.

And last be not least My special friends Wilbur Lamel, Rahjeem Collington, Donny "Lil Donny" Smallwood from the wild bunch. Tracy Lee Smallwood, Irene Morris, Brad Levin and Shawn Pruitt.

Made in the USA
Middletown, DE
13 October 2021

49927828R00116